Woodbourne Library
Washington-Centerville Public Library
Centerville, Ohio

DISCARD

W9-ACT-050

Colorful World of Animals

Peacocks

by Mandy R. Marx

Consulting Editor: Gail Saunders-Smith, PhD

Consultant: Anne R. Hobbs
Public Information Specialist
Cornell Lab of Ornithology
Ithaca, New York

CAPSTONE PRESS
a capstone imprint

Pebble Plus is published by Capstone Press,
151 Good Counsel Drive, P.O. Box 669, Mankato, Minnesota 56002.
www.capstonepub.com

Copyright © 2012 by Capstone Press, a Capstone imprint. All rights reserved.
No part of this publication may be reproduced in whole or in part, or stored in a retrieval system, or transmitted in any
form or by any means, electronic, mechanical, photocopying, recording, or otherwise, without written permission of the
publisher. For information regarding permission, write to Capstone Press,
151 Good Counsel Drive, P.O. Box 669, Dept. R, Mankato, Minnesota 56002.

 Books published by Capstone Press are manufactured with paper
containing at least 10 percent post-consumer waste.

Library of Congress Cataloging-in-Publication Data
Marx, Mandy R.
 Peacocks / by Mandy R. Marx
   p. cm.—(Pebble plus. Colorful world of animals)
 Includes bibliographical references and index.
 Summary: "Simple text and full-color photos explain the habitat, range, life cycle, and behavior of peacocks while
emphasizing their bright colors"—Provided by publisher.
 ISBN 978-1-4296-6047-1 (library binding)
 1. Peafowl—Juvenile literature. I. Title. II. Series.
QL696.G27M38 2012
598.6'258—dc22   2011000269

Editorial Credits
Katy Kudela, editor; Lori Bye, designer; Svetlana Zhurkin, media researcher; Laura Manthe, production specialist

Photo Credits
iStockphoto/DigiFox, 19
Shutterstock/David Gn, 12–13; Eky Studio, 4–5; Eric Gevaert, 1; Joan Ramon Mendo Escoda, 8–9; Laurent Dambies, 7;
     Marilyn Barbone, 15; SunnyS, 11; Zoran Mijatov, 20–21; zschnepf, 16–17
Svetlana Zhurkin, cover

The author dedicates this book to Carly in thanks for her multifaceted friendship.

Note to Parents and Teachers

The Colorful World of Animals series supports national science standards related to life science.
This book describes and illustrates peacocks. The images support early readers in understanding
the text. The repetition of words and phrases helps early readers learn new words. This book
also introduces early readers to subject-specific vocabulary words, which are defined in the
Glossary section. Early readers may need assistance to read some words and to use the Table of
Contents, Glossary, Read More, Internet Sites, and Index sections of the book.

Printed in the United States of America in North Mankato, Minnesota.
032011
006110CGF11

Table of Contents

A Colorful Display

Woosh! A peacock fans
its colorful feathers.
Bold markings look like eyes
on its tail. Peacocks can be blue,
green, white, purple, and brown.

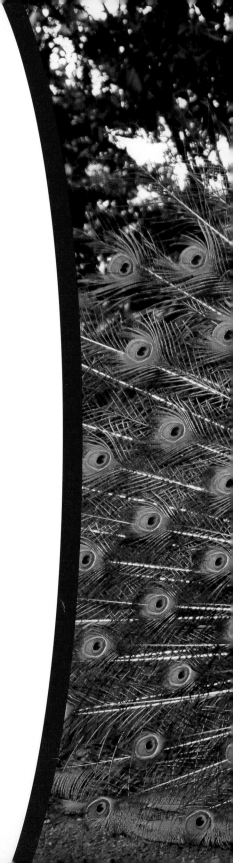

A peacock is a male peafowl.

Female peafowl are peahens.

Both male and female peafowl
are often called peacocks.

peahen

Blue and green peacocks
live in the forests of India.
Congo peacocks live in African
rain forests. Some people raise
peacocks on farms.

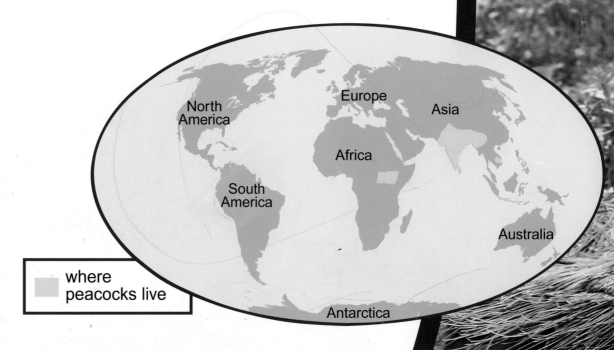

where peacocks live

North America
Europe
Asia
Africa
South America
Australia
Antarctica

Peacock Bodies

Peacocks are large birds.

Males grow to about 7.5 feet

(2.3 meters) from head to tail.

Females have slightly smaller

bodies with short tails.

Male peacocks have bright colors to attract mates. Females have duller colors that help them hide and keep their eggs safe.

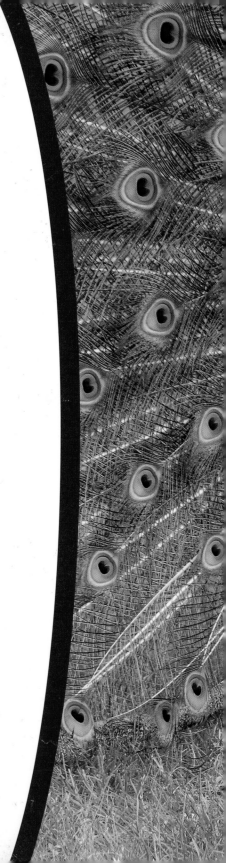

Peck, peck.

Peacocks are ground feeders.

They use their short,

strong beaks to peck at

worms, insects, nuts, and seeds.

Staying Safe

Wild peacocks live together
in groups. They sleep in tall trees
to stay safe from predators.
They call out warnings
if danger is near.

Hatching and Growing

Male peacocks mate with several females. Most females lay between five and six eggs. After 28 to 30 days, peachicks peck out of their eggs.